WRITING AND PRINTING

Written by

Steve and Patricia Harrison

Illustrated by

John Shackell, Donald Harley

Designed by

Anthony Bolton

Edited by

Lisa Hyde

Picture research by

Frances Abraham

Contents

The march of time

30,000 BC — Cave painting

3,300 BC — Writing develops in Sumer

3,000 BC — Hieroglyphs in Egypt

1200 BC — Phoenician script spreads

800 BC — Greek alphabet

BC/AD — Latin replaces Greek as Roman Empire grows

600 AD — Block printing in China

800 AD — Carolingian Minuscule abcdef in Europe

Illuminated manuscripts throughout Middle Ages

1475 — Caxton prints first book in English

1814 — Steam power presses

1845 — Rotary printers speed up printing

1938 — Biro invents ballpoint pen

1950s — Phototypesetting

1960s

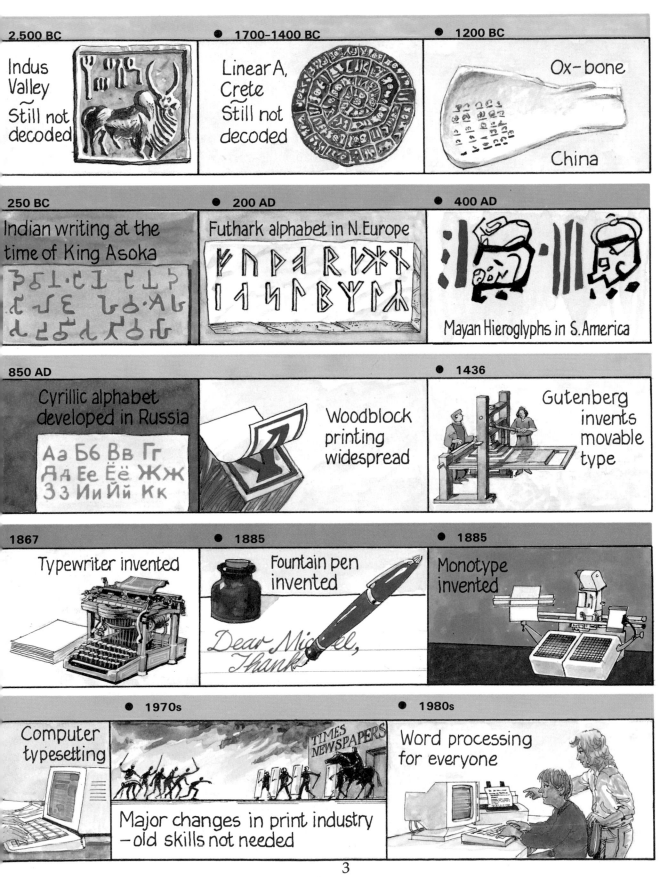

2,500 BC

Indus Valley ~ Still not decoded

1700–1400 BC

Linear A, Crete ~ Still not decoded

1200 BC

Ox-bone

China

250 BC

Indian writing at the time of King Asoka

200 AD

Futhark alphabet in N. Europe

400 AD

Mayan Hieroglyphs in S. America

850 AD

Cyrillic alphabet developed in Russia

Аа Бб Вв Гг
Дд Ее Ёё Жж
Зз Ии Йй Кк

Woodblock printing widespread

1436

Gutenberg invents movable type

1867

Typewriter invented

1885

Fountain pen invented

Dear Michael, Thank

1885

Monotype invented

Computer typesetting

1970s

Major changes in print industry – old skills not needed

TIMES NEWSPAPERS

1980s

Word processing for everyone

Cave painting and picture writing

It is part of being human to want to communicate. We do it every day whenever we speak to people and there are a variety of ways to communicate. Prehistoric people certainly spoke to each other and although they had not developed writing they could communicate by drawing and painting.

There were probably two main purposes for prehistoric art. One purpose was religious. The painting showed what the artist hoped would happen in the future. The second purpose was to tell a story of what had happened for others to see – picture stories without words.

Today we can still see some of the first prehistoric paintings in caves in France, Spain and North Africa. The idea of painting on rock is not like painting on paper. The prehistoric artists painted on uneven surfaces, so the figures they drew often had odd shapes.

These early artists had very few colours to work with. Their paints came from particular rocks which gave them yellows, reds, browns and black but no greens, blues or white. Perhaps they also used colours from vegetables or berries, but with the passage of time any remains that might once have existed have since decayed.

Painting was carried out in a variety of ways. Artists made a paint-paste by mixing coloured rock powder with grease, egg white, resin or water. They painted using their fingers and brushes.

The brushes were probably made from hair, feathers, fur or small pieces of bark tied together. Some artists blew the paint down a hollow reed.

This photograph shows a cave painting from Jabbaren, a site at Tassili n'Ajjer in the Algerian part of the Sahara desert. Like the European cave paintings it tells us something of the life of people thousands of years ago. It is also evidence that the Sahara was once a fertile land, rich in water, plant and animal life before the climate changed – a stark contrast to the Sahara today.

The world of story-telling

The cave art of Europe was painted many thousands of years ago. Art has continued to be used as a way of story-telling in modern times.

Many people still enjoy a story told through pictures, without any words being added.

Speech

Communication through speech has developed from the simple grunts of the earliest people to the kind of speaking we do today.

In the time before writing story-telling was extremely important. People would memorise their family tree and family history and pass them on verbally to their children.

There were professional story-tellers who learned stories off by heart, and then travelled from village to village telling the stories over and over again to entertain the people who lived there.

In Ancient Greece these story-tellers told wonderful tales of great cities and noble people from the past.

They described wars, journeys, shipwrecks, monsters, gods, feasts, births, deaths, great happiness and deep sorrow. For hundreds of years the stories were passed on from story-teller to story-teller and from parents to children until they were eventually written down.

Today, when we read the story of Odysseus, we are sharing an experience that Greek children enjoyed more than three thousand years ago. The difference is that we can read it for ourselves, whereas they would have heard it from a parent or story-teller.

PERSEUS FOUND THE BEAUTIFUL ANDROMEDA CHAINED UP, AS A SACRIFICE TO THE SEA MONSTER. THE WAVES PARTED AND THE BEAST EMERGED, ITS JAWS WIDE OPEN READY TO DEVOUR THE GIRL. ANDROMEDA SCREAMED AS THE MONSTER APPROACHED – PERSEUS STOOD FIRM. HE PULLED THE HIDEOUS HEAD OF THE GORGON FROM HIS SACK AND HELD IT UP. THE MONSTER WAS IMMEDIATELY TURNED TO STONE.

Activity
- Write the story of Little Red Riding Hood.
- Compare it with the same story as told by three of your friends.
- Are there any differences?
- List the stories you heard as a small child and can still remember today.

Writing begins

The more complicated life became the greater the need to keep records. As farming developed and as trade grew it became obvious that records were needed to help people remember what had been agreed or done.

The breakthrough in recording came in a place called Sumer, where the world's first writing took place. Writing developed as a way of organising and governing life in Sumer. In the first place it was used for keeping records – accounts of how many animals had been raised or objects made.

This early form of writing was rather like picture-writing. For example, the writer would count the number of oxen, draw a simple picture of an ox and next to it put a mark for each one counted. So an ox with six marks meant six oxen.

At first this writing was scratched on stone or metal with a sharp tool, but they soon thought of a simpler way of keeping records.

Sumer was rich in clay. Small tablets of wet clay were made and the writer would draw a picture into the clay. The clay could then dry in the sun or bake in an oven. It provided a permanent record, so permanent that thousands of them can still be seen today.

The clay tablet was not heavy so it could easily be taken from one place to another. It was cheap and simple to produce so there was no problem with shortages. If a mistake was made while the clay was wet it was easy to correct.

The only difficulty with clay tablets was that it proved very hard to draw circles or curves. The clay would smudge over and the writing became impossible to read.

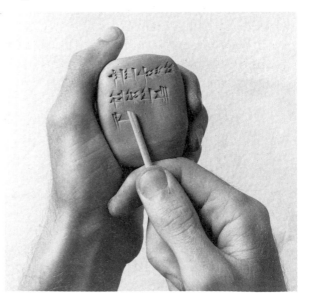

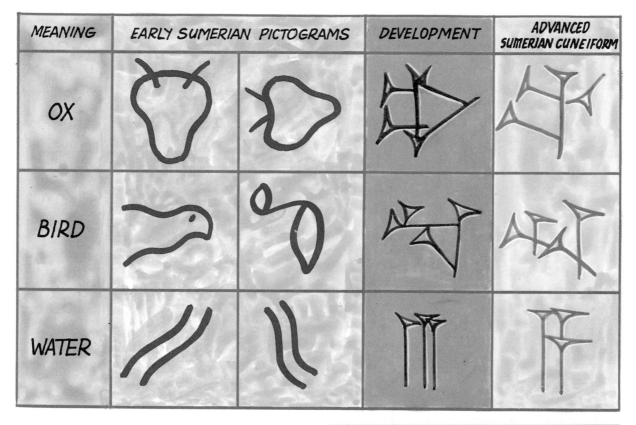

The picture language therefore had to change into pictures that only had straight lines. For some reason the scribes (writers) also began to hold the clay tablets on the side so the picture looked sideways. This is how three pictures changed over time in Sumerian picture writing.

MEANING	EARLY SUMERIAN PICTOGRAMS		DEVELOPMENT	ADVANCED SUMERIAN CUNEIFORM
OX				
BIRD				
WATER				

Scribes used a piece of bone, wood or a reed to make their marks in the clay. Their marks were wedge-shaped. It is known as **Cuneiform** from the two Latin words cuneus (wedge) and forma (shape). You can see an example of these marks above.

People gradually realised that some words don't have an obvious picture. It is quite simple to think of a picture for an ox or bird or even water, because those are things we can see. It is much harder to think of a picture which stands for an idea. The Sumerians began to have drawings for real objects and for ideas. The first type is called a **pictogram**, the second is an **ideogram**.

9

The secret of the hieroglyphs

The wonderful buildings, art, treasures and monuments of Egypt were famous all over the world. People travelled long distances to see the marvellous remains of an ancient civilisation. Many of them looked at the strange drawings painted on walls and carved in stone. Everyone knew they must mean *something* but it seemed to be a system of picture-writing whose meaning would remain a secret forever.

The key to unlocking the secret of the past was discovered by accident. French soldiers were hard at work digging at a place called Rosetta when they uncovered a tablet. This was no ordinary tablet, it was written in three different scripts – Greek, Demotic and the script of ancient Egypt – the picture-writing known as **hieroglyphic**.

Experts in foreign languages began to study the Rosetta stone looking for links between the scripts. They understood the Greek and believed that if the scripts all told the same story they would be able to gain an understanding of the hieroglyphs.

Many years passed before a Frenchman, Jean-François Champollion, finally managed to translate the hieroglyphs.

The clue lay in a small number of words on the stone which had a line drawn around them. This line, known as a cartouche, was written around the names of rulers.

Champollion guessed that the same names, written in different scripts, were inside the cartouches. The names of the rulers Ptolemy and Cleopatra were recognised in Greek. Some letters were found in both words (e.g. P). By matching up the hieroglyphs to these letters it was possible to begin the process of discovering the whole hieroglyphic alphabet.

Symbols for words

foreign land   go

Hieroglyphic writing had been used in Egypt for over 3000 years. It had gradually been replaced by Greek after the country had been conquered and ruled by Greeks.

We now know a great deal about hieroglyphic writing and therefore a good deal about the history of Ancient Egypt.

Symbols for sounds

b   w

Hieroglyphic began as simple picture-writing. The drawing stood for the object – so an owl picture stood for an owl. The problem with this kind of system was that a different picture was needed for every object in the world. Gradually pictures were developed which stood for sounds (like an alphabet) as well as objects.

Important matters were written on paper (papyrus) produced from the papyrus plant which grew in Egypt. Examples of papyrus from 5000 years ago have been discovered.

Egyptian society was very well organised and a great deal of what happened was recorded in writing. The country needed many educated writers (scribes) to keep and read these records.

Learning to be a scribe was not easy. The pupils studied long hours and they were beaten if the teacher thought they were lazy.

Pupils could not be trusted with papyrus, which was very expensive, so they wrote on bits of pottery or thin pieces of stone (called ostraca) until they were good enough to use papyrus.

Most pupils worked hard because they knew that being a scribe was a good job, well paid and comfortable and much less dangerous than being a soldier.

Early alphabets

An alphabet is different from the kinds of writing we have seen in Sumer and Egypt. An alphabet is a system of writing where signs stand for sounds in the language.

The Greeks were the first to produce such a complete system of writing, but they could not have achieved this without learning from the Phoenicians.

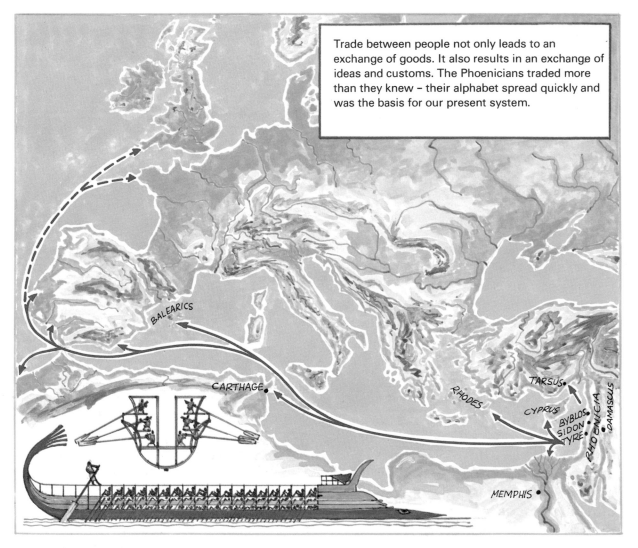

Trade between people not only leads to an exchange of goods. It also results in an exchange of ideas and customs. The Phoenicians traded more than they knew – their alphabet spread quickly and was the basis for our present system.

BALEARICS

CARTHAGE

RHODES

TARSUS

CYPRUS

BYBLOS
SIDON
TYRE
PHOENICIA
DAMASCUS

MEMPHIS

The Phoenicians were great traders. They had settlements throughout the Mediterranean and kept careful records of the goods they bought and sold.

The Phoenicians came into contact with many other peoples through trade. They learned from these contacts. It is possible to see links with Cretan, Egyptian and Cuneiform styles of writing in the Phoenician system.

The Phoenicians developed a form of writing which had no pictures but only signs representing sounds. Their alphabet had 22 letters and was used from 1200 BC. As Phoenicians travelled to other lands they would have shown their alphabet to the people they traded with.

People in Spain began to use the Phoenician alphabet (below) as did people in Greece. The Phoenicians had made writing easier for everyone. Instead of having to learn hundreds of hieroglyphs like an Egyptian writer, it was possible to learn just 22. Writing could be attempted by many more people and need not be the job of a small number of highly educated scribes.

⚐ (ʾa)	**𐤁** (b)	**1** (g)	**A** (d)	**ᴲ** (h)	**Y** (v)	**I** (z)	**目** (ch)	**⊕** (t)	**Z** (y)	**Ψ** (K)
Aleph	Beth	Gimel	Daleth	He	Vau	Zayin	Cheth	Teth	Yod	Kaph
G (l)	**𐤌** (m)	**7** (n)	**⧧** (s)	**O** (ʿa)	**7** (p)	**Γ** (ts)	**φ** (q)	**9** (r)	**W** (sh)	**+** (t)
Lamed	Mem	Num	Sameth	Ayin	Pe	Tsade	Q'oph	Resh	Shin	Tau

The Greek alphabet

The main change the Greeks made to the Phoenician alphabet was to add vowels. The Phoenicians had left it to the speakers to add their own vowels. The Greeks found this too confusing so they changed some of the Phoenician letters into vowel sounds and added others, so that all the sounds of their language were included in their alphabet.

The first two letters of the Greek alphabet Alpha and Beta gave us our word alphabet.

The Greeks did much of their everyday writing using a stylus (pointed stick) to scratch lines on wax tablets. They had the same problems using wax that the Sumerians had with clay tablets – curved lines were difficult. So Greek writing used straight lines wherever possible.

Sound	Phoenician	Greek
B	𐤁	B
K	Ψ	K
O	O	O
Q	φ	φ
R	9	P
S	W	ξ
T	+	T

Greek writing

At first the Greeks had no rules about which direction to write in. Some scribes wrote from left to right, others wrote from right to left. Some wrote from left to right, and when they reached the end of the line started the next one from right to left. The other big difference between early and later Greek writing was that they had no gaps between the words and no punctuation.

Activity
● Try to write the following message in a way that others can understand:

ONEOFTHEGOODTHINGSABOUTEARLY
NISAWYDOBONTAHTSIGNITIRWKEERG
TROUBLEFORBADPUNCTUATION

13

Chinese characters

A form of Chinese writing can be traced back 6000 years to designs on pottery and cloth from the time.

The oldest written records have been found written on the shoulder-blades of oxen.

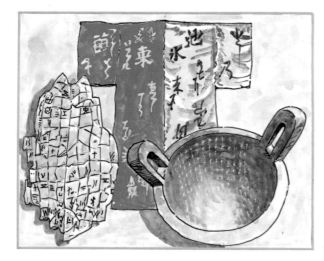

An enormous number of these shoulder-blades have been found, many with writing. More than 5000 different Chinese characters (letters/words) have been found on these shoulder-blades.

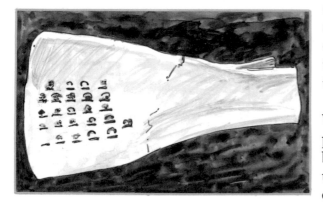

The Chinese kings and their officials believed that it was possible to forecast the future by observing certain signs. One way of doing this was to heat the shoulder-blade of an ox until cracks developed. The appearance of the cracks was carefully studied for signs about the future, which were then written onto the shoulder-blade using a writing brush.

Historical writing also began early in China. The oldest example we know of is the Shu Ching – which means 'The Book of Documents'. Some of the writing in there is more than 3000 years old.

These early writings tell us a great deal about life in China all those years ago, for example we know they used a decimal system for their numbers and that they spent a lot of time studying the planets and the stars.

Writing in Ancient China was used on pottery, bronze, tortoise shells, bamboo, wood and silk. The writers used black and deep red inks. Many official documents dating from the period before the Chinese began to produce paper have been found written on silk.

Writing on silk is a tradition that continues in China even today. Many Chinese people decorate their homes with silk hangings containing Chinese writings.

14

The Chinese writing system is **ideographic**.
Symbols (characters) stand for things and ideas.

天	想	因	土	説
SKY	*THINKING*	*BECAUSE*	*EARTH*	*SPEAK*

One problem with ideographic writing is that a different character is needed for every word in the language. There are over 40 000 characters in Chinese, and 10 000 of them are used regularly. To be able to read and write you need to know at least 2000. Only someone with a super memory could hope to know them all!

A second problem is that when a new product or idea comes in from another country which uses a different language a new character has to be produced.

In Western Europe we need to know only 26 letters to be able to read and write the words we need. The Chinese are trying to develop a simpler form of their language called Pinyin. It has only 30 characters which stand for sounds.

Waste material and rags (fibres) and water were mixed together to form a gooey substance known as pulp.

The mixture was poured onto bamboo matting which acted as a filter. The liquid seeped through but the fibre part of the pulp did not.

Once dry this material (paper) could be written on. The oldest specimens of paper discovered so far date from the time of the Emperor Han Wu-ti (141 to 87 BC).

Clues to the past

The writings of long ago can still be important for us today. They can help us to understand more about the world as it used to be. Sometimes ancient writings may have been lost for thousands of years, only to be discovered in modern times.

The Dead Sea Scrolls

Muhammad Adh-Dhib, a young boy, was travelling with his family and their animals in the mountains near the Dead Sea. They were Bedouin who knew the area well, having travelled it often.

Muhammad had lost a goat and that would mean trouble if he didn't find it. He climbed up the mountain in search of it. The sun was hot and Muhammad needed a rest. He sat under a crag for shelter and immediately noticed a hole in the cliff. A tiny hole, just big enough for a human head to poke through.

Muhammad threw a stone into the hole. He expected to hear the thud of the stone on dust but instead he heard a different sound – like that of a stone on a pot. He pulled himself up to peer through the hole and saw several large jars with wide necks.

He became afraid. What kind of creature could put those jars in there through such a small opening? It must be a devil! Muhammad was scared and ran off back to the camp as fast as his legs would carry him. That night he told an older friend what had happened. They decided to return. This time the two boys climbed through the hole and discovered a row of large pots, some with lids on them.

In one of the pots was a long scroll. The Bedouin could not read the writing so, disappointed not to find treasure, they just carried the scrolls with them on their journeys. Eventually they sold them cheaply to a trader in Bethlehem. He kept them in his shop for a while but decided, as he had to go to Jerusalem, that he would ask others to look at them there.

What Muhammad had discovered were documents dating from the time of Jesus. They gave fascinating information about beliefs and practices among Jewish groups at the time. Hidden for 2000 years, the writings helped us to understand the world of long ago and some of the ideas that might have affected Jesus and his followers.

Some old writings were regarded as untrue, old stories made up long ago. When some of them are investigated, however, they can turn out to be more than just legends.

The Great Flood

The story of Noah is well known all over the world. Archaeologists wondered if there was any evidence that such a flood actually took place, or was it simply a legend?

There existed writing from Babylon which told a very similar story known as the 'Epic of Gilgamesh'. This story caught the imagination of the archaeologist Sir Leonard Woolley. He decided to dig at the site of the great Sumerian city of Ur in a search for evidence of a flood. When he began the archaeological dig he was astonished to discover a layer of clay beneath the surface. The clay was over two metres deep and was evidence of the mud left by a flood over 6000 years ago.

Sir Leonard explained that although the area covered by the flood was not large, we must remember that the people who lived there thought it was the whole world. Once again ancient writing had helped us to find clues to the past.

Extract from 'Gilgamesh'

The gods decided that people had been so evil that they must be completely destroyed. The gods had decided to send a great flood which would cover all the land.

One god, Ea, felt sorry for one man – Ut-napishtim. He told him to start work on building a ship – big enough for his family, workers and every type of creature on earth.

Soon the rains came. It rained non-stop for six days and nights. No land could be seen. All other life was destroyed. On the seventh day the rain stopped and the boat came to rest on a rock.

Ut-napishtim sent out a dove, but it returned. Seven days later he released a swallow, which also returned. After another week he allowed a raven to fly away. The raven did not return. It must have found land, which meant that the floods were going down and land was appearing.

The gift of the Romans

Rome was greatly influenced by Greece. Greek was the language of education and business in many parts of the Mediterranean world. As writing developed in Rome the Romans simply borrowed Greek symbols, but as Rome became more powerful it gradually developed its own alphabet.

The new Roman alphabet had 23 letters.

> Some Greek letters were kept – **A B E Z I K M N O T X Y**
>
> Others were changed or added to – **G C L S P R D V F Q**

Most of the alphabets used in Western Europe today are based on the Roman alphabet. There have been three letters added to our alphabet since Roman times.

> **U** and **W** developed from the Roman **V**   **J** developed from the Roman **I**

Evidence of Roman writing is found throughout the area which was once the Roman Empire.

You will remember that the Sumerians, Greeks and others had great difficulty in writing curves. Their letters were usually straight lines with sharp edges and corners. Roman writing was different, it had curves.

This book, like all others in English, uses the Roman (Latin) alphabet but in Roman times there were only capitals.

Even letters carved on stone had curves. The mason would first draw the letter on the stone using a broad-ended pen. The carving would follow the line of the drawn letters.

The Romans also introduced the **serif**, a small finishing line which was very attractive and which is still popular today.

The Roman road system in Britain was excellent. The roads had milestones which told the traveller how far to the next town.

Many Romans who died here had tombstones erected over their graves.

The sons and a few daughters of rich Romans learned to write in school.

They used a wooden tablet which was covered in wax so that when they had practised their writing they could smooth out the wax and begin again.

They wrote with a **stylus** – a thin stick of metal, bone or ivory with a flat end for rubbing out mistakes.

'Official' documents, accounts and letters were written on papyrus.

The writer would use a pen made from a reed.

The ink was made from a mixture of soot, resin and water. It was kept in metal or clay inkwells.

Reading the runes

The Vikings were great travellers and traders. On their journeys they came into contact with many different peoples, some of whom had alphabets and detailed writing systems.

The Vikings were also enthusiastic story-tellers – proud of their family history and of their adventures, wars, victories and explorations.

Many of the Viking stories we still know of today were originally *sagas* – tales learned by heart and told on long dark winter nights, but not written down until many centuries afterwards.

The Vikings did write some things down and there is plenty of evidence of their alphabet and writing system. No one is sure where the idea for a Viking alphabet came from but it is quite possible they had seen the Greek or Roman alphabet on their travels and the idea had spread back to their homelands along the great trade routes which linked Scandinavia to the Roman cities of the Eastern Mediterranean.

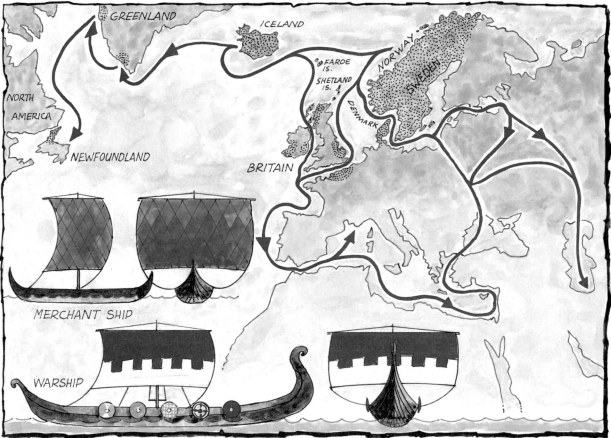

Viking explorations: dotted areas show Viking settlements.

We should remember that there was no such thing as a Viking nation. There were Vikings from Norway, Sweden and Denmark and the various groups had many differences.

Different Viking alphabets therefore developed in different parts of Scandinavia.

The letters of these alphabets were known as **Runes** so the alphabets are called **Runic**.

The Vikings passed messages and recorded events using the runes. They didn't write with pens or paint but instead they scratched their words on wood, stone and metal.

You will remember that the Sumerians and Greeks also carved their words and used straight lines because it is so much easier than carving curves. The Vikings found the same problem so the runic alphabet was made up of straight lines.

The runic alphabet is known as the Futhark alphabet because those sounds begin the alphabet.

f u th a r k h n i a s t b m l y

The oldest runic inscriptions have been found on weapons discovered in Norway. This writing has been dated to about AD 200 (1800 years ago). People's names have been found scratched on weapons and jewellery. A wide range of messages were carved on wood – including rude sayings, personal messages and trading documents.

The problem with wood is that it does not last for ever, it decays. Much of the wooden evidence has disappeared, so our best written sources for learning about Viking life are on stone and metal.

The Latin alphabet gradually became more widely used in Scandinavia and runic writing began to decline about 600 years ago. However, it is only 200 years since it went completely.

World developments

It is easy to forget that what was happening in Western Europe was not the whole story. Writing styles and technology were developing in different ways and at different times around the world.

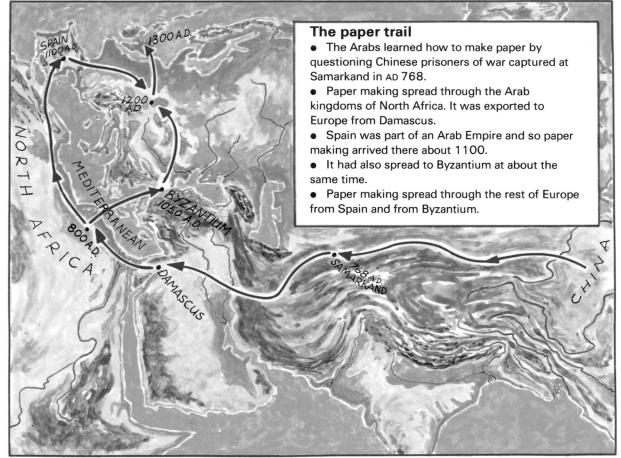

The paper trail

● The Arabs learned how to make paper by questioning Chinese prisoners of war captured at Samarkand in AD 768.
● Paper making spread through the Arab kingdoms of North Africa. It was exported to Europe from Damascus.
● Spain was part of an Arab Empire and so paper making arrived there about 1100.
● It had also spread to Byzantium at about the same time.
● Paper making spread through the rest of Europe from Spain and from Byzantium.

You read earlier (pp. 14/15) that paper making was invented in China in 100 BC. However, contacts between China and the rest of the world were not good. Ideas did not pass easily from China to the West.

The Japanese learned paper making from the Chinese in the seventh century.

The map above explains how the technology reached Europe.

Paper was first made in England in the fourteenth century but most paper used in England was imported from Europe. The first successful English paper mill was built in 1589.

Paper in – parchment out

Parchment had replaced papyrus because it was stronger, could be bound into books without being glued and lasted a long time.

Thanks to the Chinese, paper was to replace parchment as the main material for writing on in Europe from the fifteenth century to the present day.

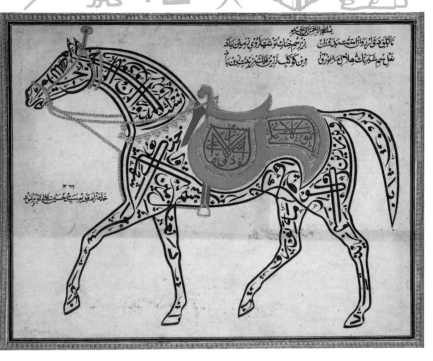

Writing has developed as a form of art in the Muslim world. There are a number of reasons for this. One is that mosques do not contain pictures of human beings or animals. Such pictures are not allowed.

It was important for mosques to have beautiful decoration. One way of creating such beauty was writing which would be pleasing to look at and remind people of the patterns that exist in the world around them.

Muslims believe that Allah spoke the words of the Qur'an to Muhammad in Arabic. In mosques throughout the world you can see beautiful Arabic script used as decoration.

This kind of writing is known as **calligraphy**. It can also be seen on copies of the Qur'an, as a pattern for textiles and as decoration on pottery.

Various forms of writing developed in the civilisations of Central and South America.

Some, like the Incas, had no writings but they did have a number system and a tradition of story telling.

The Aztecs had a writing system. They wrote on stone, cotton sheets, animal skins and on paper made from the inner bark of the fig tree. Most of their writing was in pictograms. They wrote about religion and family history and they drew maps and plans.

We do not know how far their writing would have developed because their civilisation was overturned by Spanish invaders who introduced their own alphabet and writing system.

The Mayans had the most complicated writing systems of the American civilisations. They used a system based on hieroglyphs.

Much of their writing was on the subject of time and we know a great deal about their calendar from the writings still in existence.

Changing times

From papyrus to parchment

The Romans used a large amount of papyrus. This caused a problem. The papyrus reeds which grew in Egypt were being cut down to provide the papyrus for the whole empire. A shortage was bound to happen sooner or later.

The Romans needed an alternative material and the people of the city of Pergamum produced it.

THE WOOL IS REMOVED FROM A SHEEP'S HIDE (SKIN)

THE HIDE IS SOAKED IN LIME TO REMOVE THE GREASE

THE HIDE IS THEN WASHED

IT IS STRETCHED OUT AND DRIED IN THE SUN

SCRAPING AND SMOOTHING PRODUCES EXCELLENT WRITING MATERIAL

Vellum	Advantages	Disadvantages
Vellum is similar to parchment but of even better quality. It is made from the hide of a young animal – calf, kid, lamb or antelope. Parchment is yellow, vellum is white.	• Both sides could be written on • It was easy to carry • It lasted a long time in good condition • Mistakes could be corrected by scraping the surface with a sharp pen	• It took a long time to produce • Many workers were needed • It was very expensive

From reeds to quills

Reed pens were used for writing on papyrus. Writers would sharpen the end of the reed and dip it into the ink. When the reed became blunt it could be sharpened again.

Most reed pens were 25 cm when new and would be sharpened again and again until they reached about 5 cm when they were too short for most people to use and were thrown away.

At first reed pens were also used on parchment. Later it was discovered that a better kind of pen existed for writing on parchment – the quill.

A quill is a bird's feather. The Latin word for feather is *penna*, which is where we get the words pen and pencil.

Quills, like reeds, needed sharpening regularly. A very thin line could be drawn using a quill pen if it was sharpened. A special knife was designed to cut the quill so it had a very fine point; this knife was the pen-knife, which is where we get the modern small penknife from.

From capital to small letters

The Romans had practised most of their writing on wax using a stylus. Small rounded letters are hard to write using these materials so the Romans used capital letters.

However, the Roman Empire was no longer powerful. In Western Europe it had been divided up into separate kingdoms. Fewer people could write; education was no longer as common.

In AD 768 a Prince named Charles was born, the son of Pepin, King of the Franks.

Charles grew up and his power spread. He became known as Charles the Great (or Charlemagne).

Charles believed his empire could re-create the Roman Empire of old. He felt he had a duty to educate his people. He was worried that education seemed almost to have vanished. He sent for educated people from other countries to come and work with him in his efforts.

One of these people was a man called Alcuin, from York in England.

Charlemagne ordered that all monks and priests in his empire should be able to read and write. Alcuin introduced a new style of handwriting. A style which was simple, used small letters and was clear to read. This writing is known as **Carolingian Minuscule**. Writing in small letters is easier and quicker than writing in capitals.

The Bible, religious books and the great books of Roman times were copied out in this new style all over the Carolingian Empire. Alcuin also insisted on regular spacing between words, on sentences, paragraphs and punctuation.

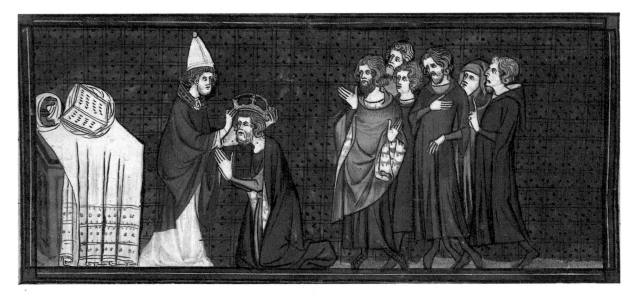

Coronation of Charlemagne.

Example of Carolingian Minuscule.

The writing habit

Charlemagne's empire soon broke up after his death but the production of books written in minuscule continued right through the Middle Ages.

The main reason for writing was to produce copies of the Bible and other religious books. These were needed in monasteries, churches and for wealthy people who wanted their own copies.

Men and women

Monks were educated but they were not the only ones who could read and write. Some rich and powerful men learned to read and write, as did some of their wives and daughters. Nuns too were often educated and some were in charge of monasteries which had both monks and nuns in them.

Teamwork

When a group of monks worked on a book they would divide up the jobs. One monk would do the writing, another the drawings, a third the coloured letters.

Because it was all done by hand the books were called **manuscripts** (*manus* = hand, *scriptum* = writing, in Latin).

We still use the word manuscript today for the first copy a writer produces, even if it is produced on a typewriter or computer.

A medieval book

Some books were produced by a team of monks, each working on a different part. At other times one monk would produce a whole book – but it might take years.

From each hide two sheets of parchment were cut – 45 cm × 25 cm in size.

These were folded in two to give four pages. Sets of four pages were put together until the book was complete. The pages were stitched together and the 'book' given a wooden frame which was covered in leather.

Rules

Among the rules which the monks had to follow when copying out the writing were:

No heating
No lighting
No talking

Why do you think these rules were important?

Later in the Middle Ages rich people became more interested in the illustrations than in the words.

They still had religious books but they probably were not very interested in the writing. They wanted to see the illustrations – which often had nothing to do with the words.

Professional artists were employed to produce these books. The monks were no longer the only ones who could read, write and illustrate.

The Domesday Book

Beautiful handwritten bibles were important to rulers in the Middle Ages, but governments always have another interest – money.

Writing was very important for rulers and their governments. Laws had to be written down, taxes collected, letters sent and details of all business recorded.

This was true for one King in particular, William the Conqueror, and resulted in the writing of one of the most famous books in history – the Domesday Book.

The Bayeux tapestry tells the story of William's invasion of England in words and pictures.

William the Duke of Normandy had invaded England in 1066. His army defeated Harold, the Saxon King, at Hastings. William was not welcome as a King to the Saxons. Many revolts took place over the next twenty years, William found he couldn't even trust the Normans – he threw his own brother, Odo, into prison on one occasion.

Gradually the land which belonged to the Saxon leaders was taken from them and given to William's Norman supporters.

In return the landowners had to provide knights for the King's army.

Every year there were problems with these arrangements. Arguments raged about who owned which land, how much it was worth, how many knights should be provided.

In 1085 William decided there had been enough arguments. He ordered a survey of England which would discover details of the land over which he ruled. How much land and property, who owned it, how many people lived there, which and how many animals they had, what was each part worth and what tax was owed on it?

The country was divided into seven circuits (parts) and William sent commissioners to each circuit.

Some of the questions asked

What is the manor called?
Who owned it in King Edward's time?

Who owns it now?	How many mills?
How many sheep?	How many fishponds?
How many swine?	How many slaves?
How many horses?	How many freemen?
How many cows?	How much wood?
How many goats?	How much meadow?

The commissioners were well educated and they completed their survey very quickly. All their written records were sent to Winchester where the King's Chief Clerk began the task of working his way through all the reports and turning them into a standard form. They carried with them any records the government already had. They arrived at the main town in each county and met the King's local representative – the shire reeve (sheriff) who would have local records with him.

They then sent for a group of men from each village or town to come and be questioned about their local area.

The answers were written down by the commissioners. Another group of villagers checked that the answers were correct.

When people were asked the questions by the commissioners they thought it was as detailed a set of questions as they were likely to be asked when they died – by God on the Day of Judgement! So they called the book the 'Domesday Book' as a sort of joke name.

The man who actually wrote the final Domesday Book was probably called Sampson – he later became Bishop of Winchester. It is written on parchment in a style which is close to Carolingian Minuscule. To help those who would have to use it Sampson underlined each heading in red and also put a red line through nearly all the place names (over 13 000).

From pen to print

Beautiful hand-copied books were produced throughout Europe for hundreds of years. Handwritten on vellum, beautifully illustrated and leather bound, they were like works of art. The problem was that it took ages to complete each book, they were difficult to produce and they were very expensive – so expensive that many were chained up to prevent them from being stolen!

Only rich people and churches could afford to own them. If more people were to have the chance to read and own books, a more efficient way of producing books was necessary. A method which would be quicker and cheaper than hand-copying.

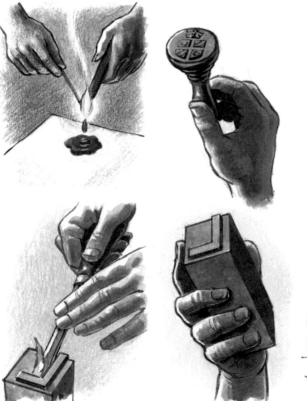

One solution to the problem had been invented in China as long ago as AD 600, but because of the poor communications with Europe it took hundreds of years before the invention was known in the West.

The Chinese had been using seals on documents for many years. Seals carried the signature of an important official and were pressed into wax on documents. It was a small step to produce a stamp which had patterns cut out of it and which when coated in ink left a print on paper.

Usually, the pattern would be cut into a block of wood – so the printing was called 'block printing'. At first only a single picture or character was carved on a small wooden block. Later larger blocks were needed as more characters were carved. Eventually wooden blocks large enough to print a whole page of writing were used.

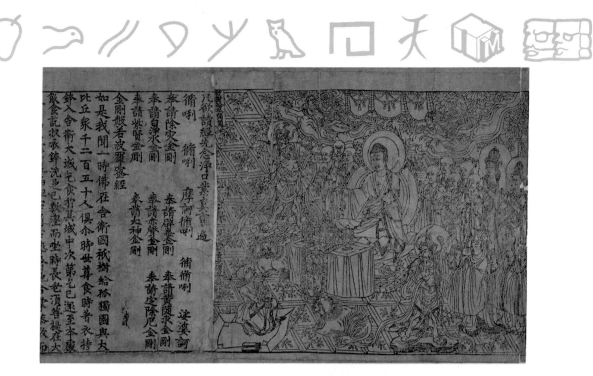

The oldest example of block printing is the 'Diamond Sutra' which was printed in China in AD 868.

The Chinese used wood and later metal block printing for producing their paper money and for printing playing-cards. The introduction of block printing followed the invention of paper making. The same thing would happen in Europe 600 years later.

No one is sure whether or not the Europeans learned block printing from links with China or whether block printing was invented separately in Europe. It is probable that the link came through playing-cards. These had been popular in China for many years and they really caught on in Europe in the fourteenth century. Everywhere people wanted to play cards. It was so popular that governments and the Church passed laws trying to ban it because some people preferred to gamble by playing cards rather than go to work. In order to supply the thousands of cards which were needed block printing was used. Perhaps the method of printing cards came from China at the same time as the idea for the cards themselves.

Block printing was then used for other purposes. Textile printing used blocks. Pictures of saints were produced in very large numbers and were much cheaper than hand painted ones. Some school books and Bibles were also produced – books which were needed in large numbers.

31

Movable type

Block printing made the mass production of books possible.

However, block printing had problems. The carving of a page into wood took a long time, and it was expensive. Once the printing was completed the wooden block was of no further use.

Wooden block prints were fine for playing cards when thousands of copies were made. It was not a good system if a printer wanted only 10 or 50 copies of a book. The cost of carving a wooden block for each page made such a book very expensive.

Gutenberg's legacy

In Europe the demand for cheaper books was growing. Inventors were hard at work trying to find a method that was cheaper and quicker than block printing.

No one is certain who invented movable type in Europe but it was probably the German Johann Gutenberg in 1436. He made a mould in which he could produce metal single letter blocks.

These letters could be grouped into

A solution to the problem had been invented in the eleventh century in China by an inventor called Bi Sheng.

He realised that if he produced a small printing block for each character he could arrange the characters in any order, print with them and then use them again in a different order.

He used clay, cut a character in it and baked it hard. He placed the clay blocks in iron frames and printed from the 'block' he had produced.

Bi Sheng had invented **movable type** but it was not very useful in China. You will remember that there are thousands of characters in Chinese. In order to have enough movable type to print in Chinese the printer would have needed thousands of small clay characters, so instead they continued to use block printing and handwriting.

Clay type as used by Bi Sheng

words, the words put into lines and the whole block covered in a new oily ink which was just right for the metal type.

His printing press was based on the wine presses used in the area. Gutenberg adapted existing technology as well as inventing the new technology of movable type. He began to print in 1450 after many years of working on his invention and after spending a great amount of money, some of which he borrowed.

Gutenberg's invention meant wood carving was no longer necessary. The metal letters could be removed, cleaned and used over and over again.

Gutenberg borrowed the money for his new invention from a man called Johann Fust. Gutenberg could not repay the loan so Fust took over Gutenberg's printing presses. Before he did, however, Gutenberg had produced a copy of the Bible using his new technology – known to the world today as the Gutenberg Bible.

Preparing to print

Hot metal was poured into a mould. Each mould would produce a block with a letter sticking out at one end. This letter was produced back to front ready for printing.

The letter blocks were put side by side to make a line and held firm in a 'stick'.

Each line was then placed into a 'galley' – a tray which held all the sticks in place.

The tray was inked and paper pressed on it. Simple but brilliant!

The first English printer

Gutenberg's invention soon spread across Europe. Many people worked with him before he lost his printing press and saw how he had produced his new method of printing. Some of them set up printing presses in other German towns. German printers travelled to many countries in Europe and started printing.

The printers had made a great technological change but they carried on some of the traditions of the handwritten manuscripts. The letter-moulds were made to produce letters which looked just like handwritten letters of the time.

The German printers used Gothic style

rein genant Malogranatus.

The Italian printers used a Roman style

Cum sonore uoce, & cum

Five printed books could be bought for the price of one hand-copied book. You might have expected everyone to prefer printed books but in fact hand-copied books were still produced. Some rich people preferred hand-copied manuscripts and were willing to pay for them. Some would not allow a printed book in their house.

William Caxton

The first book printed in English was produced by William Caxton in 1475.

William Caxton was born in Kent in southern England and spent much of his time working in various parts of Europe. He worked for Margaret, Duchess of Burgundy, in Bruges in modern-day Belgium from 1470. Margaret was the sister of King Henry IV of England and liked to read books in English which Caxton had translated from other languages. Caxton was tired of handwriting books for Margaret and other nobles to read. He complained that his eyesight was growing weaker and his hand shakier. The solution was to print the books in English using the new technology. So the first book in English was actually printed in Bruges. In 1476 Caxton returned to England and began printing in a site close to Westminster Abbey in London.

Caxton not only produced books, he also influenced the way English is spoken and written. In the 1990s we are used to hearing and reading English which can be easily understood wherever we live in Britain. We may have local dialects but we can all understand the English we hear on TV or read in the papers. In the 1440s that was not the case.

People from different parts of England spoke their own local *dialects* of English. Some dialects sounded like foreign languages to people from other parts of the country. Even if the word was the same the spelling was not fixed. The same word could be spelt in a number of different ways.

Caxton's introduction of printed books in English began to change all this.

His books were written in the dialect he spoke, the dialect known as East-Midland which included London and the eastern part of England from the Thames to the Humber. The spellings he used became widely accepted and other printers followed his example.

Canterbury Tales

The best known of the books Caxton printed was *The Canterbury Tales* by Geoffrey Chaucer. The tales are about a group of pilgrims who are on their way to Thomas à Becket's shrine at Canterbury. On the journey they have a competition to find who can tell the best story. The winner is to receive a free dinner at the Tabard Inn on their return.

Caxton's edition included drawings of the pilgrims. The example shown here is a mixture of new and old technology. The words are set in movable type, the picture is printed from a wooden block.

Activity
- Make a list of the words that are spelt the same today.
- Write the modern next to the old word.
- Write out the passage in modern English.
- Now read Chaucer's words opposite set in modern type (below) and compare it with the Gothic type he used.

A knyght ther was a worthy man
That fro the tyme that he first began
To ryden out, he loved chyvalrye
Trouthe and honour freedom and curtesye

35

The printing shop in 1600

The author sent his handwritten work (manuscript) to the printer. Inside the printing shop a team of people worked hard to turn the manuscript into a top quality printed text. Each member of the team was trained to carry out specialist tasks.

Bundles of paper being delivered for use by the printer.

The author's manuscript is pinned up so that it can be read easily.

These men are the compositors. It is their job to set type into a composing stick, make up the lines into pages and then lock them into a chase for printing.

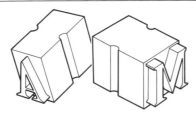

Each letter is engraved on a metal block. The blocks are placed side by side to make words.

A final check is made and the senior compositor corrects any mistakes before the printing begins.

The type has to be evenly [in]ked before it will print [pr]operly. Two inking pads are [u]sed. The ink is kept in a jug.

Printed pages are hung up to dry.

The printer uses the printing press to press a piece of paper down onto the inked type. This leaves an impression on the paper and another page is ready for drying.

The master of the printing shop makes sure that all the workers do their jobs properly.
Mistakes damage his reputation and are expensive to correct.

A young boy is employed in the printing shop. He is learning the trade; he is an apprentice.

THE
FOVNTAINE
OF SELFE.LOVE.
Or
CYNTHIAS
REVELS.

As it hath beene sundry times
priuately acted in the Black-
Friers *by the* Children
of her Maiesties
Chappell.

Written by BEN: IOHNSON.

Quod non dant Proceres, dabit Histrio.

Haud tamen inuideas vati, quem pulpita pascunt.

Imprinted at London for *Walter Burre,* and are to be
solde at his shop in Paules Church-yard, at the signe
of the Flower de-Luce and Crowne. 1601.

Diaries

All sorts of people keep diaries. Most are handwritten daily.

Diaries are an excellent source of evidence to help us understand the lives and times of people in the past. Some old diaries contain recipes, price lists, details of illnesses, marriages, births and deaths. Who knows, if you keep a diary it might be read by children in a hundred years' time who can learn all about you!

Samuel Pepys

Samuel Pepys (pronounced Peeps) had an important job in the Navy Office in London. During his lifetime England was involved in many wars and the Navy was very important. He regularly met and talked to the King.

When Samuel was at university he learned a system of writing which we call **shorthand** – letters or symbols used for words. It allows the writer to write more quickly. Pepys used it for all his writings, including his diary. It was also useful because most other people could not understand it so his diary was a secret to everyone else.

Pepys began his diary on 1 January 1660 when he was 27 and he wrote it every day until 31 May 1669. He stopped then because his eyesight had been badly affected by writing his diary by candlelight every night. The diary contains one and a quarter million words.

7 June 1665
'Today I saw two or three houses in Drury Lane marked with a red cross upon the doors and "Lord have mercy upon us" written there.'

Pepys writes of the plague in London

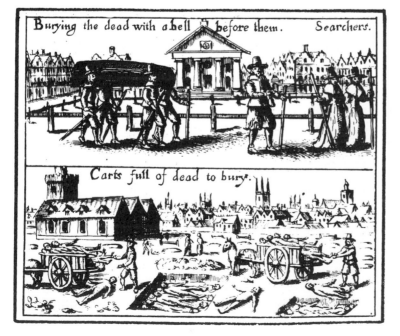

Burying the dead with a bell before them.   Searchers.

Carts full of dead to bury.

30 July 1665
'It was a sad noise to hear the bell toll so often today, either for deaths or burials. I think there were five or six.'

14 November 1665
'Captain Coche and I travelled in his coach along Kent Streete (a sad place because of the plague, people sitting sick, with plasters about them in the street, begging).'

Anne Frank

Anne Frank's diary is very different from Samuel Pepys'. Anne wrote while she and her family lived in hiding in Amsterdam because they were Jewish and this was 1942. Hitler's secret police were searching for Jews who would be sent to concentration camps and almost certain death.

There were eight people living in the rear upstairs rooms of what had been Mr Frank's office. Dutch friends kept them hidden and provided food but there was to be no leaving those rooms. No one except their closest friends should see or hear any sign of life. Anne wrote her diary in those rooms.

Dit is een foto, zoals ik me zou wensen, altijd zo te zijn. Dan had ik nog wel een kans om naar Holywood te komen.
Anne Frank. 10 Oct. 1942

20 June 1942
'Jews must wear a yellow star, Jews must hand in their bicycles, Jews are banned from trams and are forbidden to drive . . .'

6 June 1944
'"This is D-day" came the announcement over the British Radio and quite rightly . . . The invasion has begun . . . the best part of the invasion is that I have the feeling that friends are approaching . . . Perhaps I may be able to go back to school in September . . .'

25 May 1944
'This morning our vegetable man was picked up for having two Jews in his house. It's a great blow to us . . . but it's terrible for the man himself . . . the only thing to do is to eat less . . . we shall cut out breakfast altogether, have porridge and bread for lunch, and for supper fried potatoes and possibly once or twice a week vegetables or lettuce, nothing more. We're going to be hungry, but anything is better than being discovered.'

Anne never went back to school. On 4 August 1944 she and her family were arrested. On 23 September they were packed into cattle-trucks and sent to Auschwitz – a camp where many Jews were sent to be killed. The family was split up. Anne and her sister were sent to Belsen camp in November. There they both died in the spring of 1945.

Like so many others Anne was a victim of racial hate. Yet through her diary we feel as though we still know her today and her writings remind us of how important it is for all people to stop anything like Anne's fate happening again.

The technology of change

Braille

Louis Braille was born in France in 1809. At the age of three Louis was blinded in an accident. As he grew older he realised that the only way he could know what was in books was if someone else read them to him. Louis decided there must be a way of making it possible for blind people to read. Their eyes might not see but the rest of their senses were working.

By the time he was 16 Louis had begun to develop a system of writing which could be read by touch.

Each letter of the alphabet was given a pattern of raised dots. By learning what each pattern stood for the blind person could learn to read. We call this system Braille. The Braille alphabet is printed here. It not only contains dots for the alphabet but also for some very common words and punctuation. The pattern is made up from 1 to 6 dots.

Remember – in this book they are shown as dots. In a book produced for the blind they are raised dots which can be felt. So the printed book allows people to read with their fingers.

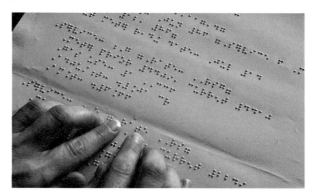

Braille alphabet

A B C D E F G H I J K L M

N O P Q R S T U V W X Y Z

What does this message say?

Writing

People continued to use quill pens for their handwriting right up to the middle of the nineteenth century.

They were gradually replaced by steel nibs but at first the steel nib was placed on the quill. It was only later that nib-holders were produced as well.

There were thousands of designs, shapes and sizes for the new pens. However, there was still the problem that the nib had to be dipped into the inkwell every few seconds.

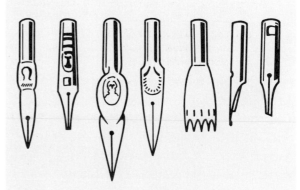

Pen-and-ink writing increased greatly in 1840 when a national system of posting letters for the price of one penny was introduced. Letter writing became much more popular and sales of nibs grew rapidly.

There was another 'boom' in the production of pens when schools stopped using slate pens and writing slates and switched to pen and paper writing. If you speak to adults about their schooldays many will be able to remember the inkwell and the 'dip' pen they had to use. Some will have vivid memories of what happened if you blotted your paper with ink!

Lewis Waterman

Fountain pens had been invented but they were always flooding.

One day an insurance salesman called Lewis E. Waterman was trying to sell an insurance policy to a rich customer in New York City. Lewis persuaded the man and gave him a form to sign. The customer borrowed Lewis's fountain pen and started to sign his name but the pen flooded and ruined the form.

Lewis went away to find another form and while he was away a rival salesman arrived and sold the customer a different policy!

Lewis Waterman decided that would never happen to him again. He spent the next three years inventing a fountain pen which did not flood. He became rich as a fountain pen manufacturer and never needed to sell another policy. You can still buy 'Waterman' pens in shops today.

Ink

The Chinese used ink made of soot, gum and water but it was not good quality and easily rubbed off the paper after a time.

In the Middle Ages all sorts of recipes were used including a mixture of iron ore and oak apples.

Ballpoints

The first ballpoint was invented by George and Lazlo Biro in Hungary in 1938. Many people still call ballpoint pens 'biros'.

This invention was improved in the 1950s when a special quick-drying ink was invented. Before then the ballpoint could be quite messy. Ballpoint ink is much thicker than bottled ink.

There is a small ball at the tip of the pen which takes the place of the point in a fountain pen.

Inside the pen there is a tube full of ink and as you write the ball picks up ink from the tube and rolls it onto the paper. When the pen is not being used the ball acts as a stopper and this prevents the ink escaping or evaporating.

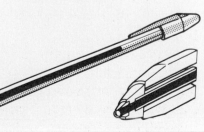

The power of print

Printing has helped to change the world. New ideas were written down, printed and made available to large numbers of people quickly and cheaply.

In the early sixteenth century nearly all Christians in western Europe accepted the Pope in Rome as head of the Church. Earlier attempts to challenge the power and teachings of the Church had failed.

A new challenge came when Martin Luther, a German priest, decided to openly criticise the Church and to question the actions and powers of the Pope and priests. Luther wrote down his objections in Latin and in 1517 he nailed them to the door of the church at Wittenberg. His friends and supporters had Luther's writings translated into local languages and printed on the new presses. His ideas spread like wildfire.

Between 1517 and 1520 Luther's writings sold more than 300 000 copies, and remember this was at a time when most people could not read!

Luther's teaching resulted in the splitting of the Christian Church of western Europe. It led to a Europe divided into Roman Catholics and Protestants. The printing presses played an important part in that change.

Propaganda from a Lutheran writer printed in 1520 at Basle. The animals are supposed to be the Pope and Cardinals at Rome.

Many governments both in the past and today are afraid of allowing people to read what they like. Often governments try to control what is printed.

In Germany in the 1930s the Nazi party came to power. They tried to control the way people thought. One way of doing this was to destroy all the books the Nazis did not approve of. Books by Jews, Socialists and many others were burned on great bonfires.

In 1990 there was a revolution in Romania. The country's dictator, President Ceausescu, was overthrown and shot. During his time as President he had controlled the press in Romania. It was even illegal for a person to own a typewriter or a copier.

Changing public opinion

Printing presses have been used to bring about changes in the law. The two propaganda posters shown here were used this century in Britain. In 1900 only men could vote. Women decided to do something about it but the government would not listen. Many protests followed. Women were thrown into prison. When they refused to eat they were force-fed.

Gradually the protest and arguments put pressure on the government and in 1918 women over thirty years old were given the vote. It was only in 1928 that women were given the same right as men to vote at twenty-one.

Printing has made mass advertising possible. Now you can see famous logos like the Coca-Cola sign all over the world, printed on posters, in magazines, on tiles, on metal, on cans, glass and even T-shirts. The power of print includes the power to sell goods as well as spread ideas.

Read all about it!

The Gutenberg technology remained the basic method of printing until the early nineteenth century. Changes came when steam power was used to drive the presses. Frederick Konig, working in Germany, invented a *cylinder* press which was steam powered. The cylinder could print four times faster than a flat printing frame.

Monotype invented

power presses

Speed was further increased when rotary presses were invented. Now four rollers fed paper across a central cylinder. Once again four times as many pages could be printed in the same period.

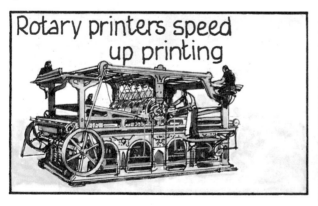

Rotary printers speed up printing

In 1884 and 1885 the production of type was speeded up with Linotype and Monotype machines. Now a keyboard could be pressed and brass matrices (or moulds) set in place, ready for molten metal to be pumped in to produce type for printing.

The modern print revolution

In the 1960s a new revolution began in printing. Computer technology meant it was no longer necessary to have 'hot metal' printing. Journalists could type in their copy (the words they write) and it was ready to print once a plate was made using photosensitive materials.

This made printing quicker, easier and cheaper, but thousands of people were no longer needed in the printing industry. Workers tried to halt the changes. Strikes were called. Some newspapers closed down. There was fighting outside newspaper offices. In Britain the 1980s marked a great change. Most newspapers went over to the new technology.

Today's story today

When a story 'breaks', the editor sends a reporter to the spot. She collects information from witnesses.

Using a lap-top computer she can type out the 'copy' which will appear in the paper.

The story is put alongside other items on a page layout. The page is photographed, a printing plate is made which goes for printing.

She then sends her 'copy' to the newspaper using a telephone and modem. The 'copy' appears on screen and can be edited at once.

As the pages are printed they are folded, put together as newspapers and wrapped in bundles.

In no time at all they are on the streets ready for the public to buy and read.

How this book was made

'I'm Lisa Hyde, the editor of this book. When we decided to publish a book on Writing and Printing it was my job to choose the authors. I asked Steve and Patricia Harrison to write it. When they send me their copy (the text they write) I check it, perhaps change some of it and then have it typeset. I have to make sure the project stays on schedule so we publish on time.'

'We are Steve and Patricia Harrison. Once we had signed the contract we began our research. We visited museums and libraries in Britain and Europe. We used a wide range of books and art sources. We produce one double page at a time. We wrote all the words, chose the photographs and decided what the artwork should be. The publisher pays us a royalty – which means we receive money for each book sold.'

'My name is Tony Bolton. I'm the book's designer. I chose the artists, John Shackell and Donald Harley, and they produced the artwork for this book. Frances Abraham, the picture researcher, provides Steve and Patricia with a range of photographs to choose from. I bring the copy, photographs and artwork together and make up the page layout ready for printing.'

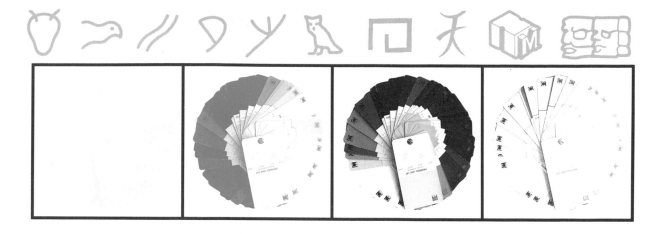

Colour printing is a complicated process. All the photographs and artwork go through a machine called a scanner. This separates the original artwork into four photographs of different colours.

The printer makes four different printing plates, one for each of the four colours. These plates are put on rollers. Paper passes through the printing press and is printed on by each of the four rollers. The four colours combine to make all the colours you see in this book.

The first copies to be printed have to be checked carefully just in case any mistakes have been made in the printing process. The printers who produced this book are based near Bristol in England. Their machinery also cuts and folds the printed paper ready for final binding.

The pages are glued or stitched into sections and the sections are glued into the covers. This book was produced in hardback and paperback editions. Hardbacks last longer but they are more expensive than paperbacks.

It's great to see the book finally produced. It has taken nine months from start to finish, but now it can go into bookshops and schools.

Index

Published by BBC Educational Publishing,
a division of BBC Enterprises Limited,
Woodlands, 80 Wood Lane, London W12 0TT

First published 1991
© Steve and Patricia Harrison/BBC Enterprises Limited 1991

Paperback ISBN: 0 563 34787 2
Hardback ISBN: 0 563 34788 0

Typeset by Ace Filmsetting Ltd, Frome, Somerset
Colour reproduction by Daylight Colour, Singapore
Cover origination in England by Dot Gradations
Printed and bound by BPCC Hazell Books, Paulton

Photo credits
Page 5 Robert Harding Picture Library; 8 BBC Enterprises; 9 Ancient Art & Architecture Collection; 10 & 11 British Museum; 13 Robert Harding Picture Library; 16 Ancient Art & Architecture Collection; 21 ATA, Stockholm; 23 Victoria & Albert Museum *photo* John Webb/BBC Enterprises; 25 *both* British Library; 27 Bibliothèque Nationale, Paris; 29 Public Record Office; 31 *top* British Library. *bottom* Science Museum *photo* Bridgeman Art Library; 33 British Library; 34 & 36–7 *main picture* Mary Evans Picture Library; 37 *bottom right* John R. Freeman/BBC Enterprises; 38 *top* National Portrait Gallery, *bottom* Magdalene College, Cambs.; 39 Popperfoto; 40 Zefa Picture Library; 42 *top* Folger Shakespeare Library *bottom* Imperial War Museum; 43 *both* Mary Evans Picture Library; 44–5 *all* Lancashire Evening Post; 46 *all* BBC Enterprises; 47 *both* BPCC Paulton Books Ltd.

Front cover   *Main picture* Mary Evans Picture Library. *Inset top left* British Museum, *top right* Bibliothèque Nationale, Paris, *bottom right* ICL.

The authors would like to thank Carol McNulty, Linda Edmondson and John East.